House Windows Vocabulary

A Glossary of Definitions

By William J. Saunders

ISBN-10:1984126393
ISBN-13:9781984126399

About This Book

Be prepared. Whether you are buying, selling,
installing, or in any way involved with household
windows, you will fare much better if you know
and understand the terminology.

Consider this reference book to be a field guide to
the terms that will show up in transactions and
specifications, and prepare you to understand them
and be in better control of the decisions you will be
making.

Being informed will help prevent mistakes and
losses – And save money.

AAMA (American Architectural Manufacturers Association) is a professional group that develops product performance standards and provides certification for windows. Look for their Silver Certification Label for thermal performance, or their Gold Certification Label for thermal performance, and basic structural, air and water performance.

AIA (American Institute of Architects) is a leading professional membership group for licensed architects.

ANSI (American National Standards Institute) is the voice of the U.S. standards and conformity assessment system. Its Mission Statement: "To enhance both the global competitiveness of U.S. business and the U.S. quality of life by promoting and facilitating voluntary consensus standards and conformity assessment systems, and safeguarding their integrity."

ASME (American Society of Mechanical Engineers) is a professional membership group that enables collaboration, knowledge sharing, career enrichment, and skills development across all engineering disciplines.

ASTM International was formerly **American**

Society for Testing and Materials and is a professional group and a globally recognized leader in the development and delivery of international voluntary consensus standards.

Acoustic Attenuation is a measure of the level of sound transmission that is reduced through windows.

Air Locks or Vent Latches restrict the ability of a **Single Hung** or **Double Hung** window sash to be opened more than a few inches to provide some semblance of safety and weather protection.

Apron is a decorative section of trim molding lying flat against the interior wall below the window **Stool** (sometimes called the interior "window sill").

Aluminum Windows are typically less efficient due to temperature transfer through the frame. Thermal breaks can help.

Annealed Glass is a typical, standard float glass slowly cooled to increase strength. The glass tends to break into dangerous splinters, which is why tempered glass is recommended or required for certain window applications, i.e., for safety when window bottoms are close to the floor.

Argon is a denser-than-air inert gas inserted between the panes of glass in a double pane window **Insulating Glass Unit (IGU)** to slow thermal transfer through the window.

Asbestos is a mineral fiber used in many building materials, including siding and insulation. Exposure can lead to illnesses like lung disease, according to studies and subsequent regulations.

Astragal is a piece of trim molding used to cover the joining gap between a pair of closed doors or windows.

Awning Window is hinged at the top or the sides, and the bottom edge opens outward giving the appearance of an awning.

Background Check is used by agencies and some employers to investigate a person's history for criminal records, to protect the public and to help avoid liability.

Balance is a mechanism to ease the lifting, lowering, and holding a sash in an open position in **Single Hung** and **Double Hung** windows. There are many different types and styles with varying degrees of durability and dependability. They include block and tackle, channel, friction, spiral, coil, constant force, and hybrids.

Balance Rod is used to apply tension in spiral type balances in **Single Hung** and **Double Hung** windows.

Balance Shoe is used to attach the window balance to the sash in some **Single Hung** and **Double Hung** windows.

Balance Winding Tool is used to adjust the tension of spiral balances in some **Single Hung** and **Double Hung** windows.

Bay Window is a set of 3 windows protruding out at 30 or 45 degree angles. A typical arrangement is a center **Picture Window** with a **Single Hung** or **Double Hung** window on each side. The choice between 30 and 45 degree angles is dependent on protrusion limitations due to plantings, walkways or soffit depth. It may be less costly if the **Soffit** can be used as a roof instead of constructing a new roof over the **Bay Window** assembly.

Bevel is an angle cut for a more finished look, or for joining one piece to another piece of material.

Blinds are interior window treatments, or are sometimes installed between the glass panes during the manufacturing process.

Block and Tackle Balance is a type of counterbalance with pulleys and cord on some **Single Hung** and **Double Hung** windows to ease opening and closing the sash, and to hold the sash in place when open.

Bow or Warp in Window Glass is distortion from heating and cooling during the manufacturing process that can cause the glass to bow or warp.

Bow Window is similar to a **Bay Window** but it protrudes at lower angles (10 degrees is common) for a curved rather than angular look. These typically have **Casement Windows** and / or **Picture Windows**. Like a **Bay Window**, this window assembly needs a roof constructed if the **Soffit** can't serve that purpose.

Breather Tubes are usually less than six inch long aluminum cylinders used to equalize barometric pressure differences in high altitude windows.

Brick Header is usually a length of angled steel used to support a course of bricks over a window.

Brick Mold is an exterior frame molding around most windows and doors.

Building Code Regulations are standards enforced by local, state and other agencies

Building Permit is often required to ensure that construction or remodeling work meets the applicable building code regulations. They often require a fee and a follow-up approval.

Bulb Seal is a compression seal used on some windows for improved weatherproofing and energy efficiency.

Butt Casing refers to vertical side trim members (side casing) that have flat ends to join with the horizontal top casing and / or bottom member (**Apron** or **Stool**). The joint is called a butt joint as opposed to a miter (diagonal) joint.

Butyl is a synthetic rubber sometimes used to gain an airtight seal and used on some window spacers.

Cames are the decorative divider strips, sometimes made of lead, which are adhered to join window glass pieces (or imitate that look) for decorative effects (Leaded Glass) (Church Glass).

Canadian Fog Box Test is accepted in the industry as an indicator of potential seal failure caused by the chemical reactions of different materials.

Capillary Tubes are typically aluminum or steel tubes, about twelve inches long, used to equalize barometric pressure in high altitude windows.

Capping or Wrapping or Cladding or Flashing usually applies to a painted or **PVC** coated aluminum that covers and protects window caulk and brick mold or other external window trim. In some parts of the country it's called **Wr**apping and in other parts it's called **Capping, Cladding** or **Flashing**.

Cardinal Glass is a glass brand of the company, Cardinal Glass Industries.

Casement Window is hinged at the left or the right edge, and usually cranks outward. Some models swing at the jamb and some pivot inches from the jamb to allow enough room to reach out and wash both sides of the window when it is open.

Casement Arm Operator is a hinge mechanism used to open and close a **Casement Window** by turning a crank handle.

Caulk is a substance used to help seal cracks and spaces. There are many different types to use for windows, so it is best to follow the window manufacturer's recommendation.

Chamfer is a bevel cut, usually 45 degrees, to give a finished appearance or to join a piece to another piece of material.

Charging Tool adjusts the tension on the spiral balances in some **Single Hung** and **Double Hung** windows.

Check Rail refers to the horizontal rails that meet in the center of **Single Hung** and **Double Hung** windows (**Meeting Rail**).

Chemical Fog is caused by materials (chemicals) used within an **Insulating Glass Unit (IGU)** that can produce fogging between the panes of glass. Tests like the **Canadian Fog Box Test** are performed to analyze various materials.

CIE is the **International Commission on Illumination** also known as the CIE from its French title, the Commission Internationale de l'Eclairage and is devoted to worldwide cooperation and the exchange of information on all matters relating to the science and art of light and lighting, color and vision, photobiology and image technology.

Circle Top Window has a flat bottom rail and a

curved top, like a semi–circle, and may or may not have grids / grilles.

Circle Window is a round window with or without grids / grilles.

Clad is a metal or some other protective material used to cover the window frame surface.

Cladding is a term that usually applies to a painted or **PVC** coated aluminum that covers and protects window caulk and brick mold or other external window trim. In some parts of the country it's called **Wrapping** and in other parts it's called **Capping** or **Flashing**.

Clarity Is a measure of an **Insulating Glass Unit (IGU)** visibility without obstructions to the view.

Clear Glass is window glass without tint or **Low E** coating.

Coil is a description of roll-packaging the **PVC** coated aluminum used to cap/wrap.

Cold rolled is a metal forming process that increases material strength and improves the finish.

Colonial Grids or Grilles describes a pattern of vertical and horizontal bars installed in or on a window. The Colonial Style imitates windows made in the days when only small panes of glass could be manufactured and larger openings were filled with a number of small, framed windows.

Commercial Use is a term that may include rental properties and multi–family dwellings in addition to commercial properties like offices and storefronts. Most replacement window warranties have clauses that limit coverage for **Commercial Use** properties.

Composite Window uses a material formulation as an alternative to wood, metal and vinyl window frames.

Condensation is a phenomenon that can occur on windows when water vapor condenses into liquid on the window surface. It is usually due to high humidity on one side of the window when the surface of the other side of the window glass is below the dew point.

Condensation Rating (CR) is a **National Fenestration Ratings Council (NFRC)** resistance rating that measures water build–up on windows on a scale or 0 to 100 where higher is better. A higher resistance means less water build–up.

Condensation Resistance Factor (CRF) is a pass/fail rating from the **American Architectural Manufacturers Association (AAMA).** A higher number means higher resistance to condensation.

Conduction is a term describing heat and cold transfer from one object to another object, such as from one pane of glass through a spacer to another pane of glass.

Consumer Products Safety Commission (CPSC) is a government agency with a goal of protecting the public against unreasonable risks of injury from consumer products through education, safety standards activities, regulation, and enforcement.

Contractor is a General Contractor or some other type of person or company engaged in projects for hire.

Convection is a term that describes heat and cold transfer between places such as through the air or gas between panes of glass.

Corner Keys are fasteners used to join the corners of window frames and / or window spacers together.

Coped Joint is machined to fit the contours of pieces being joined together such as those in a window trim corner.

Cottage Style Window is a single or double hung window with a lower sash that is larger than the upper sash, usually at a 60% bottom / 40% top ratio.

CPSC (U.S. Consumer Products Safety Commission) is a government agency with a goal of protecting the public against unreasonable risks of injury from consumer products through education, safety standards activities, regulation, and enforcement.

Craftsmanship is a term that is often used to describe the window installation process. A Craftsmanship Warranty usually refers to the Installation Warranty.

Crank Handle is used to open and close most casement, awning, and jalousie windows.

Cripple is the name of the support studs that are located both under the rough window sill and above the window header.

Cullet is recyclable glass waste.

Damping Gas is used in double pane windows to reduce heat convection currents and improve energy efficiency.

Date Code is used by some manufacturers to label their products to show when they were fabricated.

Deed Restrictions are things that are and are not allowed to be done with real property. They are usually called **Deed Restrictions** and are listed in the Real Property Deed.

Desiccant is a substance to help keep some thing or some area dry by absorbing moisture. That is one of its functions in the manufacture of **Insulating Glass Units (IGU)**. Another function is the ability to maintain a low dew point within the **Insulating Glass Unit (IGU)** over a period of time.

Dew Point is the temperature at which water vapor in the air condenses into liquid.

Divided Lite Window is the term for a grid/grille pattern that gives the appearance of connected small windows by using both interior and exterior grids / grilles. The **Full Divided Lite Windows** have an additional grid / grille inside the panes of glass between the interior and exterior grids / grilles to give a more realistic imitation of old **Colonial Style** windows.

coating on a pane of glass. Think of emissivity as absorption. The less absorbed by a reflective substance, like silver, the more reflected. A Low Emissivity (**Low–E**) coating on a window pane will reflect more radiant energy away from it than is absorbed and emitted.

Energy Efficiency is usually indicated by **U Factor** and **Solar Heat Gain Coefficient (SHGC)** for windows.

Energy Star is a **U.S. Environmental Protection Agency (EPA)** voluntary program which helps businesses and individuals save money and protect our climate through superior energy efficiency.

Energy Tax Credit – **(ETC)** is a credit offered by government agencies to homeowners in return for purchasing energy efficient products.

EPA is the **U.S. Environmental Protection Agency** whose mission is to protect human health and the environment.

Excluder is also called a Draft or Draught Excluder, and is a weatherproofing seal for windows and / or doors.

Extension Jamb is a part used to compensate for a jamb depth that is wider than the standard for a particular replacement window.

Extrude is a manufacturing process that can produce products with intricate cross sections and superior strength.

Extruded Aluminum is an alternative process to roll–form aluminum in windows and insect screens. The extruded product is said to be stronger and more durable, while the roll form product is usually less expensive to fabricate and to purchase.

Eyebrow Window has a flat bottom rail and a curved (arc) top. Compared to a **Half Round Window**, the **Eyebrow Window** can have long vertical sides (legs).

Fading is caused by UV radiation through windows that can discolor window treatments, furniture, carpets, paint and art.

Fascia is a decorative and protective board running horizontally under a roof edge, attached to the roof rafter ends, and joining to the **Soffit**. Gutters are usually attached to the fascia boards to catch runoff from the roof.

Fenestration is an architectural term for window and door openings in a building.

Fillet is a name for a thin piece of molding used as a separator of or an accent to other moldings.

Fin Seal is a thin, flexible insulating strip used on some windows and doors for energy efficiency.

Finite Element Analysis (FEA) is a test for potential **Insulating Glass Unit (IGU)** seal failure.

Flashing is material, usually sheet metal or aluminum, used at joints and junctures to prevent water seepage into a structure. This term also applies to a painted or PVC coated aluminum that covers and protects window caulk and brick mold or other external window trim. In some parts of the country it's called **Wrapping** and in other parts it's called **Capping, Cladding** or **Flashing**.

Float Glass is the name of glass with uniform thickness which is achieved by floating molten glass on molten metal. It is said to be of a better quality than plate glass.

Fluted Molding has decorative ribs (flutes) running the length of the molding.

Fogging –occurs when condensation develops between the panes of glass in an **Insulating Glass Unit (IGU)** usually caused by seal failure, resulting in air and moisture entering the cavity.

Forced Entry Requirements (FER) is an **AAMA** designation refers to the ability of a locked door or window to resist forced entry.

Franchise is a business arrangement for purchasing the use of a logo, other business rights and support marketing to sell products and services.

French Casement Window has no center **Mull or Mullion** and allows a clear view when open.

French Door is a double door that swings in or swings out to open.

Frieze is a decorative design that is usually horizontal and sometimes constructed above windows and doors.

Full Divided Lite Window has a grid / grille pattern that gives a more realistic imitation of connected small windows by using a filler grid / grill between the glass panes aligned with interior and exterior grids / grilles.

Full Frame Window is a new-construction type of window, complete with a frame to be installed in a rough opening. These are used as replacement windows when the original frames are unusable or unrepairable.

Full Screen – The insect screen shields an entire window as opposed to a half screen which is often used in **Single Hung** and **Double Hung** and most sliding windows. Half screens are becoming more common for their convenience and better partial view.

Fusion Weld is a manufacturing process where the window parts to be attached are melted and joined for better structural integrity.

Gable describes the triangular roof and dormer style design which allows rainwater to flow down and away, and snow not to accumulate easily.

Garden Door is a set of two joining hinged doors, sometimes called swing or **French Doors**.

Garden Window is a miniature greenhouse-like structure, usually installed over a kitchen sink, to allow for a combination of plantings, light, view and ventilation.

Gas is denser than air and gas, such as Argon and Krypton, is used between double and triple pane windows and doors for better energy efficiency.

Geometric Window is a non–rectangular shaped window (Triangle, Trapezoid, etc.).

GANA is **The Glass Association of North America** and provides the organizational structure for addressing the needs of a diverse trade membership.

Glass Deflection is an **ASTM International** Standard for determining wind load resistance. This is especially important for residences in storm–prone areas.

Glass Logo identifies the manufacturer and the date of manufacture, which is helpful when ordering replacement parts.

Glaze is a name for material, like putty, which seals the window glass in the frame.

Glazing Bead holds or seals the glass in place inside a window or door frame.

Greenhouse Gas is a term that encompasses a number of gases that trap heat in the atmosphere. They include Methane (CH4), Carbon dioxide (CO2), Nitrous oxide (N2O), and Fluorinated gases.

Grids are also called **Grilles** or Bars, and are used in or on a window or door to give it a particular style (Colonial, Prairie, Victorian, etc.).

Grilles are also called **Grids** or Bars, and are used in or on a window or door to give it a particular style (Colonial, Prairie, Victorian, etc.).

Half Round Window has a semicircle window design where the height equals one half of the diameter.

Half Screen shields half of a **Single Hung** or **Double Hung** window and most **Sliding** windows for convenience and a better partial view.

Hard Coat Low–E reflective metal is joined to glass in its molten state (Pyrolytic), and is more durable and less expensive than **Soft Coat Low-E** but has a bluish tint. Since Soft Coat Low-E is applied in a vacuum, Hard Coat is the only option for single pane Low-E windows.

Hardware describes the parts, such as lifts and locks, used in or on windows and doors,

Header is the support beam above a window or a door, which is usually made of a 2x6, 2x8, or 2x12 section of lumber.

Heat–Strengthened Glass is a heating process that yields glass about twice as strong as untreated glass. The manufacturing process is similar to **Tempered Glass** but differs in the cooling cycle, which makes tempered glass about four times as strong as untreated glass.

Hexagonal window is a window with six sides.

High Altitude Windows require special construction, including breather or capillary tubes, to prevent seal failure and glass breakage due to high barometric pressure.

Historic Areas in some cities have designated areas with special, restrictive **Building Codes**.

Homeowners Association (HOA) is a type of regulatory organization found in certain communities.

Hopper is the name for a basement window hinged at the bottom or sides that tips in for ventilation.

Hurricane Resistant Windows are designed to help maintain building envelope integrity in severe weather.

IG is **Insulating Glazing (IG)** and refers to **Double Pane** or **Triple Pane** windows.

IGCC –is the **Insulating Glass Certification Council, a** trade organization offering 3rd Party Certification of **Insulating Glass Units (IGU)** for seal durability & gas content in compliance with the **ASTM** E 2190 standard.

IGMA is the **Insulating Glass Manufacturers Alliance**, the world's leading organization on the engineering and manufacturing of insulating glass.

IGU is an **Insulating Glass Unit**, an assembled and hermetically sealed window assembly of two or three panes.

Ingress is the clearance needed to enter a window or door opening in an emergency. Building and fire codes dictate the dimensions.

Insert Window is a complete window (frame and sash) to be inserted into an existing window frame or pocket.

Installation Warranty covers the **Craftsmanship** of the installation work for some period of time.

Insured Contractor refers to liability protection for injury and property damage. Coverage may or may not extend to crew and helpers.

Insulating Glass Unit is the **IGU,** an assembled and hermetically sealed window unit that fits within a frame.

Insulation is used to slow the passage of heat, cold

and air.

Inswing are doors and windows that swing in to the room.

IR (Infrared Reflection) is a process to measure and reduce **Solar Heat Gain**.

IRC is the **International Residential Building Code**, a regulatory specification.

J.D. Power is a global marketing information services company providing performance improvement, social media and customer satisfaction insights and solutions.

Jalousie Window has parallel, horizontal, louvered panes in a frame and opens outward for ventilation.

Jamb is each of the vertical legs of a window or door frame.

Jamb Liner covers a Jamb cavity and, in some cases, the Balance mechanism.

Keeper is the stationary part of a window sash locking mechanism.

Key Stone is the center piece of a decorative external header.

King Stud is a full length vertical member attached to the end of the window header.

Krypton Is a denser than air inert gas between the panes of glass to slow thermal transfer.

Laminate Finish is applied over the vinyl window for a wood-like appearance.

Laminated Glass has a laminate adhered to the glass to prevent dangerous shattering.

Lead Paint Safety requires an **EPA** approved test for the presence of lead paint on pre–1978 homes. If present, certified installers and special procedures are required for window replacement projects.

LEED is the Acronym for **Leadership in Energy and Environmental Design (LEED)** and is a program to provide third–party verification of green buildings.

Lifetime Warranty means different things to different people and companies. Read the fine print to determine the real meaning of "Lifetime" in warranty documents.

Lift Rail is the horizontal frame member used to raise or lower a sash in **Single Hung** or **Double**

Hung windows.

Limited Warranty has many meanings. Read the fine print for the meaning of "Limited" in the warranty documents.

Lineal is an exterior trim accessory for windows and doors.

Lintel is a horizontal structure installed over two vertical supports of a window or doorway for a decorative appearance.

Lock and Keeper are found in **Single Hung** and **Double Hung** as well as **Sliding** windows. The set includes a moveable lock and a stationary keeper.

Low–E is the **Low Emissivity** metallic coating on **Low-E** windows. Think of emissivity as absorption. The less absorbed by a reflective substance, like silver, the more reflected. A **Low Emissivity (Low–E)** coating on a window pane will reflect more radiant energy away from it than is absorbed and emitted.

Low–E2 is advertised as two metallic layers in multi–pane windows.

Low–E3 is advertised as three metallic layers in

multi–pane windows.

LSG is an acronym for **Light to Solar Gain** and is the ratio of **VT (Visible Transmittance)** to the **SHGC (Solar Heat Gain Coefficient)**, meaning VT / SHGC = LSG.

Meeting Rail is where the horizontal rails meet in **Single Hung** and **Double Hung** windows (check rail / lock rail).

Mesh Screen is a name for a window insect screen. They are typically made of fiberglass or aluminum.

Metal Window usually refers to steel or aluminum windows. It also refers to the metal nailing flanges on new construction windows when they are replaced.

Miter Joint is a style of joining two 45 degree cuts to make a 90 degree corner.

Mortise and tenon is a right angle joining of a tenon pin and a mortise hole.

Mull is a vertical or horizontal divider between windows.

Mullion is a vertical or horizontal divider between windows.

Muntin is a flat or sculpted grid or grille separating individual panes of window glass.

Nailing Flange is used on full frame, new construction windows to attach the windows to the exterior of the house. These are normally sawed through when installing replacement insert windows and may entail a labor charge.

NFRC is the acronym for the **National Fenestration Ratings Council** and is an **American National Standard Institute (ANSI)** Accredited Standards Developer (ASD). It develops and administers comparative energy and related rating programs for fenestration products.

Obscure Glass is a glass treatment that provides limited visibility.

Octagonal Window is a window with eight sides.

Opaque Glass is a glass treatment that provides limited visibility.

Oriel Style Window is a **Single Hung** or **Double Hung** window with a larger upper sash than lower sash usually at a 60% upper / 40% lower ratio.

Outswing are windows and doors that swing out of a room.

P–1 Test is a rigorous **ASTM International** seal failure test for **Insulating Glass Units (IGU)**.

Painting can void a window or door warranty. Check the warranty documents for restrictions and exceptions.

Pane is the piece of glass within a window frame.

PAR is an acronym for **Photosynthetically Active Radiation**, the spectral range for better plant photosynthesis.

Parting Strip is also called a **Parting Bead** and, usually in a vertical recess or gain in each jamb, separates the upper and lower sash in a **Single Hung** or **Double Hung** window.

Patio Door is usually encased glass and opens to a patio, porch or deck.

Permit refers to a **Building Permit** and is often required to ensure compliance with local **Building Codes**.

PGC International is **Protective Glazing International** and represents manufacturers of protective glazing products and systems, suppliers to these manufacturers, consultants and testing organizations.

PGMC is **Primary Glass Manufacturers Council**, a trade group.

Picture Window is fixed and non–operating.

PIB (Polyisobutylene) can be used as a window seal to lessen gas leakage from between double and triple pane windows.

Pile Seal is weatherstripping that is woven and extruded.

Plumb is a measure of straight up and down, and perpendicular to a horizontal surface.

Pocket or Insert Window is a fully framed window that fits within an existing window frame for easier and less disruptive installation.

Prairie is a decorative **Grid / Grille** style that frames the perimeter of the window glass.

Primed indicates that that a paintable surface is prepared for finishing.

PSF is an acronym for **Pounds per square foot**. PSF is a measurement of pressure.

PSI is an acronym for **Pounds per square inch**. PSI is a measurement of pressure.

Pulley is a grooved wheel used in a block–and–tackle type of window balance system.

PVB Interlayer (Polyvinyl butyral resin) is an insulating compound used in windows.

PVC (Polyvinyl Chloride) is the primary material in vinyl windows and frames.

R–Value is a measure of resistance to heat loss. A higher R-Value is a better insulator.

Rabett (Rebate) is a groove cut in the edge of a piece of material, like wood, for joining purposes.

Radius is equal to one–half the diameter of a circle.

Rail is a horizontal member of a window sash frame.

Replacement Window – is a window to replace an existing window as opposed to a new construction window. Replacement windows are sometimes called insert windows when they are self–contained window units designed to replace the old sash and fit within the old frame. There are situations where the entire old unit, sash and frame, are replaced with full frame replacement windows – sometimes referred to as a "full rip."

Reveal is a small gap left between the window trim or casing and the window jamb for a more appealing look and to mask irregularities.

RHG (Relative Heat Gain) is the total amount of heat transfer through a window.

Rolled Form Aluminum is a less expensive alternative to extruded aluminum windows.

Rollers are used in Gliding Patio Doors and some **Slider Windows**. They range in quality from plastic to stainless steel with ball bearings.

Rough Sill is the horizontal member at the bottom of the window rough opening.

Safety Glazing meets **Consumer Products Safety Commission (CPSC)** and / or **Safety Glazing Certification Council (SGCC)** standards for glass breakage safety.

Sash is a moveable window panel, vertical, horizontal, outward or inward.

Sash Tensioning Tool is used to adjust spiral tube balance rod tension.

Screen (Insect screen) is usually fiberglass or aluminum mesh, in an aluminum frame.

Seal Failure causes inert gas to leak out of the **Insulating Glass Unit (IGU)** and is replaced by air. It usually results in fogging between the panes.

Security can be an issue so some windows are manufactured to be impact resistant with that goal.

SGCC is the **Safety Glazing Certification Council.** SGCC is a non–profit corporation, established in 1971 by manufacturers of safety glazing products, building code officials, and others concerned with public safety.

Shim is the flat or tapered wedge or spacer to fill gaps between windows and frames.

SHGC is **Solar Heat Gain Coefficient** which is the solar radiation that enters as heat. Lower is better.

Sill is the horizontal exterior sloped or flat surface under a window pane frame, or a door.

Single Pane windows have low energy efficiency when compared to most modern windows, which have two or three panes for much better energy efficiency.

Single Strength Glass is typically 3/32" thick.

Slider Window has two or three panels and slides horizontally.

Soffit is the under-covering from the fascia board to the exterior siding.

Soft Coat Low–E is a reflective metal coating applied (Sputter coated) on glass in a vacuum. This process is more expensive than Hard Coat but has better light transmission. Due to the need for a vacuum, the Soft Coat is only used on the interior of **Insulating Glass Units (IGU).**

Solar Heat Gain is solar radiation that enters through the window as heat.

Sound Transmission Class (STC) has ratings that range from 18 (least) to 38 (most) amount of sound blocked.

Spacer is the component that separates panes of glass within the frame in an **Insulating Glass Unit (IGU).** It acts as a moisture barrier, gas seal, insulates against edge condensation, and allows for thermal expansion.

Spandrel Window is a triangular–shaped window between the arc of another window and its rectangular corner.

Spline is used to place and hold an insect screen in a groove or channel in its frame.

Spring Balance is a window balance spring mechanism that aids in raising and lowering single and double hung window sash.

Square has four 90 degree angles and four equal length sides.

Square Feet can be determined by multiplying the length times the width in inches and dividing by 144, or by multiplying the length in feet times the width in feet.

Spectrally Selective products block select wavelengths to reduce solar heat gain.

Sputter–Coated Low–E Glass is a reflective metal coating applied (**Soft Coat**) on glass in a vacuum. This process is more expensive than Hard Coat but has better light transmission. Due to the need for a vacuum, the Soft Coat is only used on the interior of **Insulating Glass Units (IGU).**

STC (Sound Transmission Class) ratings range from 18 (least) to 38 (most) amount of sound blocked.

Starburst Grid Pattern is a window design with radial spokes extending up from the bottom center within a semicircle arc.

Stile is a vertical section of the window sash frame.

Stool is the flat horizontal section on the interior of a window, often, mistakenly called the window sill.

Stop (Stop Bead) is the molding piece that stops the window from falling in or out of the frame.

Storm Windows have been band aid approach to energy efficiency with single pane windows installed outside existing windows to slow thermal transfer.

Straight Line Geometric Windows are Octagon, Rectangle, Trapezoid and Triangle shaped.

Strain Pattern is an apparent irregularity, but not a defect, that occurs when glass is cooling.

Structural Integrity is an indicator of the physical performance of a window under stress.

Stucco is often used as a decorative plaster–like finish on and in a building.

Stud is a vertical support in frames such as walls and around window openings.

Sunburst Grid Pattern is a window design with radial spokes from a bottom semicircle upward to a semicircle arc.

Sunstar Grid Pattern is a window design with radial spokes from bottom center upward through two semicircles.

Tax Credit (Energy) is sometimes offered by governmental agencies for energy saving purchases.

Tempered Glass tends to break without shattering into sharp shards and splinters. It is heat strengthened and rapidly cooled in the manufacturing process and is about four times as strong as untreated or annealed glass, and usually qualifies as safety glass.

Thermal Barrier is an insulator, such as gas between window panes to reduce heat flow.

Thermal Break is an insulator, such as gas between window panes to reduce heat flow.

Thermal Conduction refers to the physical transfer of heat such as a through the glass of a window.

Thermal Convection refers to the transfer of heat through its environment (air, gas).

Thermal Equilibrium (Equalized temperature) is the goal as heat flows from warmer to cooler.

Thermal Insulators reduce heat flow due to conduction and convection.

Thermal Performance is a certification metric for windows.

Thermal Radiation refers to electromagnetic transfer of heat through a surface or unit.

Thermal Window Film helps reduce radiant heat gain through a window.

Tilt Latches are used to open, tilt and close the window sash for cleaning.

Tilt Wash Window typically refers to **Double Hung** windows that tilt in for cleaning.

Transom is a window above a window or a door.

Trapezoid Window is a non–rectangular window that is often used in homes with sloped ceilings.

Trimmer Stud is a vertical member alongside the

king stud that supports the window header end.

Triple Pane Window is an **Insulating Glass Unit (IGU)** with three panes of hermetically sealed glass.

U–Factor / U–Value is the formula for heat flow rate escaping through a window. The range is 0.15 to 1.20 and lower is better. It represents the energy efficiency of the whole window, not just the glass.

UI (United Inches) is the sum of the width plus the height of a replacement window.

UV (Ultraviolet light) is electromagnetic radiation.

Vent latch stops the sash from opening more than a small amount for ventilation.

Vinyl is a polymerized resin produced for various products in various applications, including window frames and components..

Vinyl Windows are an alternative to wood, metal and composite windows.

Virgin Vinyl advertised to contain no recycled material that may contain impurities.

VLT (Visible Light Transmittance) is like **VT**

(**Visible Transmittance**) but is usually used when describing auto window film specifications.

VT (**Visible Transmittance**) is a measure of the amount of visible light passing through glass.

Warranty advice is "Always read the fine print."

Wash Assist is a tabs or other mechanism used to actuate tilt-to-wash windows.

Weather Seals are used on some windows and doors for energy efficiency.

Weep Holes allow trapped water a way to escape from window frames.

Weight Chase is a cavity within the jamb for concealing the balance weight.

Wet Glazed is a better water-proofing process around the glass edges than the dry-glaze process.

Windload is a window dimension limit based on **ASTM International** Standards for extreme weather conditions.

Window 6.3 is a standard for Complex Glazing System Modeling.

Window Casing comes in Clam Shell, Colonial,

or other molding styles.

Window Seal Failure causes the gas to be replaced by air and moisture.

Window Seal Failure Rate varies greatly by manufacturer but the high–end is about 1.5%.

Window Seal Stress on the spacer seal can cause vapor leakage and glass breakage.

Window Stop is a strip of molding that stops the window from falling in or out of the frame, and is removed to allow the sash to be replaced.

Window Treatments are decorative, protective, and energy-saving materials and include curtains, drapes and blinds.

Wood Window Frames are now often clad, capped, or wrapped with aluminum, vinyl, or other material for weather protection, energy efficiency, and durability.

Wrapping or Capping or Cladding or Flashing – usually refers to a painted or PVC coated aluminum that covers and protects window caulk and brick mold or other external window trim. In some parts of the country it's called Wrapping and in other parts it's called **Capping, Cladding** or

Flashing.

Other Books by William J. Saunders

How To Buy New Windows For Your Home
The Home Improvement Guide
ISBN 9781982091507

How To Buy Replacement Windows For Your Home
The Home Improvement Guide
ISBN 9781495257582